DON'T KEEP THE CHANGE

GEN ALPHA'S BLUEPRINT TO MASTER MONEY

DON'T KEEP THE CHANGE

GEN ALPHA'S BLUEPRINT TO MASTER MONEY

Shaurya Jain

Worldwide Published by

Pendown Press

PENDOWN PRESS LLP
An ISO 9001 & ISO 14001 Certified Co.,
Regd. Office: 3767A, Kanhaiya Nagar,
Tri Nagar, Delhi-110035
Ph.: 8130886000, 9650072927
E-mail: info@pendownpress.com
Branch Office: 1A/2A, 20, Hari Sadan, Ansari Road,
Daryaganj, New Delhi-110002
Ph.: 011-45794768
Website: PendownPress.com

Edition: 2025

ISBN: 978-93-6338-786-7

Layout and Cover Designed by Pendown Graphics Team
Printed and Bound in India by Thomson Press India Ltd.

CONTENTS

ACKNOWLEDGEMENTS

First and foremost, I want to thank the universe for all the inspiration and strength to bring this book to life. The universe wills, and events happen. I'm so grateful for all the opportunities and the people you surround me with.

I want to thank my amazing parents, **Mr. Anand Jain** and **Mrs. Darshana Parmar Jain**. You've been my biggest cheerleaders, guiding me with your love, wisdom, and values. I wouldn't be where I am today without you, and I'm so lucky to have you as my role models.

A heartfelt thank you to **Mr. Arvind Jain** and **Mr. Neelesh Khandelwal** for writing the forewords for this book. Your words of wisdom and encouragement have added so much value, and I'm truly honored to have your support.

A huge shoutout to **Mr. Dinesh Verma**, CEO of Pendown Press, and his incredible team. Your guidance and ideas helped make this book so much better. Thank you for believing in me and supporting me every step of the way!

Lastly, to my friends and family—thank you for being there for me through it all. Even if I couldn't mention everyone's name, please know you have a special place in my heart. Your encouragement and support mean the world to me.

This book wouldn't have been possible without all of you. You gave me the confidence to dream big and make it happen.

Shaurya Jain

FOREWORD

I've been lucky to have had the joy and privilege of seeing Shaurya grow up into a young man with an extremely evolved analytical acumen, and I think everyone who reads this book will definitely benefit immensely.

I really like this book because it speaks directly to two very important groups: Gen Alpha and their parents. It's a bridge between generations, built to tackle one of the most universally challenging conversations: money.

For the younger generations, you're growing up in a world that's more connected, digital, and fast-paced than ever before. You're tech-savvy, creative, and already changing the world in ways that no other generation has before. Knowing how to manage money gives you an advantage over 96% of your peers.

Parents, you're raising kids in a time of endless opportunities and challenges. It's tough to know where to start when teaching financial lessons, especially when the landscape keeps changing. This book is your toolkit. It's here to help you empower your kids with timeless wisdom, tailored for the modern world.

Here's to a journey of learning, growth, and financial freedom.

Arvind Jain

Pride group

Construction I Hospitality I NBFC

FOREWORD

As a Chartered Accountant, I've observed one universal truth: financial literacy is a subject that very few families cover with their children systematically.

This is why I'm thrilled to be a part of this book. Shaurya has grown up in a business family household. As a child author, he is able to speak directly to Gen Alpha and their parents about his experiences through his book.

For all families, it is necessary to understand that the opportunities are immense. Children today are part of a generation that will witness India's rise as a global economic powerhouse. But with these opportunities come complexities. Parents have the chance to pass down timeless principles like discipline, delayed gratification, and the importance of giving back, while also equipping their children to thrive in a world of fintech apps, market volatility, and global commerce. This book is the perfect guide for navigating this balance.

This book is a very good read for all families. I hope Shaurya continues to write and be the bridge between Gen Alpha and parents for more money conversations.

Neelesh Khandelwal

Founding Partner

Shah Khandelwal Jain & Associates

INTRODUCTION

Personal finance for children, parents, and teens is an essential aspect of financial literacy that focuses on equipping younger generations with the knowledge and skills necessary to understand their money effectively. Parents of young children also need to understand how to educate them and have meaningful conversations about money at home. Let's be real—nobody gets rich counting their pennies!

What is the right age? What is the way? How do you approach this with children for a positive impact? As technology reshapes our lives, the way we approach personal finance must evolve too. This book was born from a simple yet pressing question that my parents had: How can we prepare the next generation, Gen Alpha, to thrive financially while bridging the gap between them and me?

The discussion about why it is important to earn and value enough, though my family was privileged, happened often, every time I wanted to procrastinate or not make the effort. The answer lies in knowledge and communicating openly about everything at home, and adaptability. Gen Alpha is growing up in a unique era—one dominated by digital currency and instant access to everything online, including global markets. They are the pioneers of tomorrow, but without the right tools, navigating these financial waters can feel overwhelming.

I also developed a mobile application called **Stash** for this sole purpose—to help families do this easily.

The significance of personal finance education lies in its ability to prepare young individuals for future financial challenges. Research indicates that children who receive financial education are more likely to develop healthy financial habits, such as saving for emergencies and planning for future expenses.

Various strategies, including age-appropriate instruction, interactive learning, and real-life applications, can enhance the effectiveness of financial literacy programs. Moreover, collaboration between parents, schools, and community organizations plays a pivotal role in reinforcing these concepts at home and in educational settings.

Notably, challenges such as the complexity of financial concepts, the influence of consumer culture, and the inconsistent availability of financial education programs in schools can hinder effective teaching.

CHAPTER - 1

Start Small, Dream Big:
The Early Bird Advantage

Figure 1

Many people believe that learning about money is something that should happen later in life. But in reality, teaching children about personal finance from a young age (starting as early as 4) can make a huge difference and create a foundation for lifelong financial success. Kids are naturally curious and eager to learn at this age, which makes it the perfect time to introduce basic financial concepts in a fun and engaging way.

The Early Bird

Starting early helps children build strong financial habits. These habits can shape their entire lives. Children who learn about money at a young age are more likely to:

➢ Make smart spending decisions.

➢ Develop financial ethics early.

➢ Understand the value of saving.

➢ Avoid debt as they grow older.

Just like learning to ride a bike or read, understanding how to manage money is a skill that takes time and practice. The earlier children begin, the more confident and capable they become in handling financial decisions later in life.

The Brain's Development in Early Childhood

At the age of 4, children are rapidly developing their cognitive abilities—like problem-solving, decision-making, and understanding cause and effect. Teaching them how to manage money during this critical stage helps them grasp abstract concepts like saving and spending. The earlier they start learning, the more natural it becomes.

Key Concepts:

➢ **Ages 5–10:** Saving for toys, learning needs vs. wants.

➢ **Ages 11–15:** Budgeting, basic investing.

➢ **Ages 16–18:** Minor banking, managing allowances.

How to Introduce basic financial concepts

Here are simple, practical ways to introduce financial concepts to very young children:

1. Using **Visual Tools:** Create three jars for "Spending," "Saving," and "Sharing." These jars help children visually organize their money and understand its different uses. Whenever they receive money—whether as gifts, rewards, or pocket money—they can divide it among these jars:

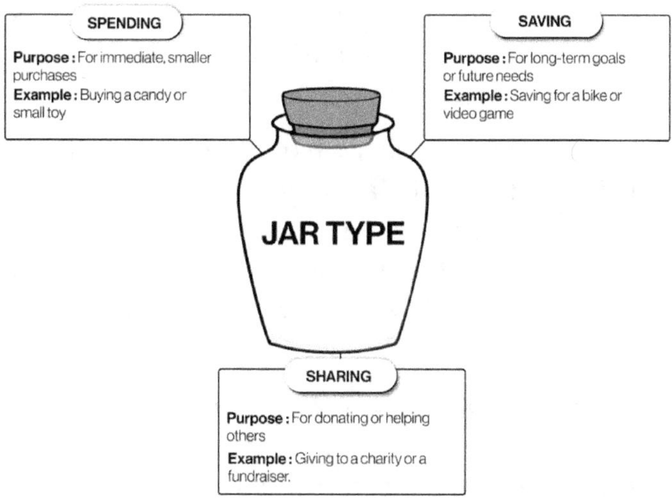

Figure 2

2. **Introduce Counting Money:** Start by teaching children to recognize and differentiate between various coins and notes. You can make it more engaging by playing games like "shopping" where they can practice counting money, adding totals, and giving change. This not only helps them understand the value of money but also sharpens their basic math skills in a fun way.

3. **Role Play:** Set up a pretend store at home. Let your child pick out items (like toys or snacks) and "pay" for them using real or play money. This simple activity helps them understand that money is exchanged for goods or services.

Story: "The Two Brothers and the Candy Jar"

Once upon a time, there were two brothers, Arjun and Varun. One day, their grandmother gave them ₹100 each to spend however they wanted.

Arjun ran to the store and bought a huge bag of candies. He was so excited, but within a few days, all his candy was gone. He felt a moment of joy but soon realized he had nothing left.

Varun, on the other hand, put his money into three jars—₹50 in his Spending jar, ₹30 in his Saving jar, and ₹20 in his Sharing jar. A few weeks later, Varun still had enough money saved to buy a toy car he had wanted for a long time. Not only that, but he also donated to a local animal shelter, which filled him with a sense of pride and happiness.

When Arjun saw how much joy Varun had from saving and sharing his money, he realized something important: it's not about how fast you spend your money, but how wisely you manage it. The lesson stayed with him, and from that day forward, Arjun decided to use jars too.

Parent and Child Activity

Parents and children can create their own jars and start practicing together. You could also have a weekly "budget meeting" where the child can discuss what they've saved, what they've spent, and how much they've set aside for sharing.

CHAPTER - 2

Money Is for Everyone:
Breaking the Gender Myth

Historically, society has unfairly pushed the narrative that men are better at managing money than women. This belief stems from outdated traditions where men were the breadwinners, while women were relegated to household duties. But times have changed. Today, women are not only managing their households but also leading Fortune 500 companies, running financial empires, and reshaping the global economy.

MALAVIKA HEGDE
CEO, Café Coffee Day

Figure 3

Let's debunk the myth that boys are biologically engineered to understand finance better. Studies have shown that financial aptitude is not tied to gender. Boys and girls are equally capable of learning, understanding, and excelling in financial literacy when given equal opportunities. Skills like budgeting, investing, and saving are taught—not innate. If anything, society's expectations—not biology—have limited girls from pursuing financial knowledge in the past.

Boss Ladies of the Finance World

To prove that finance is for everyone, let's look at some real-world examples of women dominating the financial sector:

➤ **Janet Yellen:** As the first woman to serve as both Chair of the Federal Reserve and U.S. Treasury Secretary, Yellen has made groundbreaking contributions to global economic policy.

➤ **Abigail Johnson:** The CEO of Fidelity Investments, one of the largest asset management companies in the world, Johnson oversees trillions of dollars and inspires women everywhere to lead in finance.

➤ **Oprah Winfrey:** While not a traditional financial executive, Oprah's business acumen has turned her into a self-made billionaire. Her story shows how understanding money can empower anyone to succeed.

These women have proven that finance isn't reserved for one gender. They've shattered glass ceilings and paved the way for the next generation of financially savvy girls and boys alike.

One of the most important steps in breaking the stereotype is teaching boys and girls about money equally. When we present finance as a skill anyone can master, we create a more inclusive society where everyone has the tools to succeed.

Parents and educators play a crucial role here. Instead of giving boys toy cash registers and girls dolls, why not encourage both to play money games? Why not involve daughters in family budgeting discussions just as much as sons? These small shifts can dismantle the idea that finance is a "boy's world."

When both boys and girls understand finance, society benefits as a whole. Women who are financially literate make better decisions for their families, contribute to economic growth, and are less likely to face poverty in retirement. Men, too, benefit when they view women as equal financial partners. Together, they can build stronger, more secure futures.

My personal favourite story is cafe coffee day. Cafe Coffee Day's story took a dramatic turn after the tragic death of its founder, **V.G. Siddhartha,** in 2019. Burdened by debts exceeding ₹ 7,000 crore, the company faced an uncertain future. Siddhartha's wife, **Malavika Hegde,** stepped in as CEO, determined to honor her husband's legacy. Through strategic debt restructuring, operational efficiency, and rebuilding trust with stakeholders, she successfully steered the company back toward stability. Today, Cafe Coffee Day stands as a testament to resilience, leadership, and a commitment to overcoming adversity.

Creating a Level Playing Field

One of the most important steps in breaking the stereotype is teaching boys and girls about money equally. When we present finance as a skill anyone can master, we create a more inclusive society where everyone has the tools to succeed.

Parents and educators play a crucial role here. Instead of giving boys toy cash registers and girls dolls, why not encourage both to play money games? Why not involve daughters in family budgeting discussions just as much as sons? These small shifts can dismantle the idea that finance is a "boy's world."

When both boys and girls understand finance, society benefits as a whole. Women who are financially literate make better decisions for their families, contribute to economic growth, and are less likely to face poverty in retirement. Men, too, benefit when they view women as equal financial partners. Together, they can build stronger, more secure futures.

Finance has no gender. It's not about biology, and it's not about tradition—it's about access, education, and mindset. The world needs more financially empowered individuals, regardless of whether they're boys or girls. So, whether you're a young boy reading this book or a young girl, remember: the world of finance is yours to conquer.

CHAPTER - 3

Money Habits That Stick:
Your Lifetime Toolkit

Have you ever heard the saying, "Old habits die hard"? It's true, especially when it comes to money. The habits we develop in childhood often stay with us for life. That's why it's important to guide children early on to build good financial habits that set them up for success.

How habits shape your financial future:

Imagine money as a tree. If you plant the seeds properly and take care of them, they will grow into something strong and fruitful. The same applies to financial habits. Teaching children to save regularly, plan their spending, and think before they buy helps them understand how to manage money effectively.

Here's an example:

➢ **Impulsive Spending Habit:** A child who spends all their pocket money the day they receive it will struggle to buy things they really want.

➢ **Saving Habit:** A child who saves part of their money learns to prioritize long-term goals over short-term pleasures.

Talk to children about making smart choices, like waiting a little longer to buy something better or saving for something meaningful instead of spending on something they don't truly need. These lessons can shape their mindset for life.

Tracking spending

Do you ever wonder where your money goes at the end of the month? Children feel the same way when they realize they've spent their money too quickly. Introducing them to the idea of tracking their spending can make a big difference.

Here's how to make it fun:

➢ Create a **spending journal** or use a simple notebook where they can write down everything they buy.

➢ Use stickers or colors to categorize expenses: snacks, toys, or savings.

➢ Turn it into a game—who can track their spending better this week?

By tracking their money, children start to understand patterns in their behavior. They'll see, for example, how buying small candies every day adds up to a bigger cost than they expected. This awareness helps them think twice before making impulsive purchases.

The snowball effect of savings

Saving money isn't just about putting coins in a piggy bank—it's about creating opportunities. Teach children how small savings can grow into something big over time.

Figure 4

For example:

➢ If a child saves ₹ 10 every week, they'll have ₹ 520 in a year.

➢ If they add birthday or holiday money, the amount grows even faster!

You can make this lesson visual and exciting:

1. Use a transparent jar or a chart to track their savings progress.

2. Set a goal, like saving for a toy, book, or even a special outing.

3. Celebrate their achievement once they reach their target—it shows them the rewards of patience and persistence.

Just like a small snowball rolling down a hill becomes bigger as it collects more snow, saving consistently adds up to something larger. This also introduces the idea of compounding, where saving and reinvesting money can lead to exponential growth in the future. That's the "snowball effect" for you!

Involve the Whole Family

Financial habits don't have to be a solo journey. Parents and children can learn together, creating a positive environment for financial education. For example:

➢ Have a **family budgeting day** where everyone discusses their spending and savings goals.

➢ Share personal stories—how parents saved for their first bike, first phone, or a family vacation.

These activities not only teach money management but also strengthen family bonds.

Activities for Parents and Children

Choose a country and research its money habits. Create a poster or presentation about what kids in that country do to save or earn money. (For example, Kakeibo is a century-old Japanese technique for budgeting).

CHAPTER - 4

Needs vs. Wants:
The Smart Saver's Guide

The distinction between needs and wants is vital. Needs are basic requirements such as food, shelter, and healthcare, while wants are non-essential items that enhance the quality of life. Make a list of wants and evaluate what is a necessity. Develop a conscious approach to spending. Open communication about these concepts fosters better understanding and responsible financial behaviors. So **Wallet, meet your new best friend: self-control!**

1. Needs:

These are essential items required for day-to-day living and well-being. Needs include food, shelter, clothing, school supplies, healthcare, and utilities like electricity or water. Without meeting these needs, it becomes difficult to survive and maintain a healthy lifestyle. Needs are non-negotiable and should be prioritized over anything else.

Example: A school uniform, a healthy lunch, and notebooks are needs. Without these, it's difficult to attend school and learn effectively.

2. Wants:

Wants are the things that are nice to have but are not essential for survival or immediate well-being. Wants include toys, video games, movie tickets, and junk food. It's easy to confuse wants with needs, especially when advertisements make everything seem like a "must-have." This is where children learn the power of self-control and the importance of delayed gratification. It's okay to enjoy these things, but they should never come before meeting their needs.

Example: A new toy, an extra video game, or an ice cream after school, a date are wants. These are things you might enjoy, but you don't absolutely need them right away. It's important to remember that wants are things that bring temporary happiness., and they may not contribute to long-term well-being or success.

3. Savings:

Saving means setting aside money for future use, whether for a short-term goal (like buying a bicycle) or long-term purposes (like a college education). It also prepares the family for emergencies, helping to build a safety net for unplanned expenses. By introducing the concept of saving early, families can build an understanding that money is not just for spending but also for securing their future.

Example: Saving part of their earned money for a bigger item, like a bicycle or a school trip, is important. If they spend all their money on small wants, they may not have enough for something important or exciting in the future.

The 50-30-20 Rule

Now that we understand the concepts of needs, wants, and savings, let's explore how much should be allocated to each category.

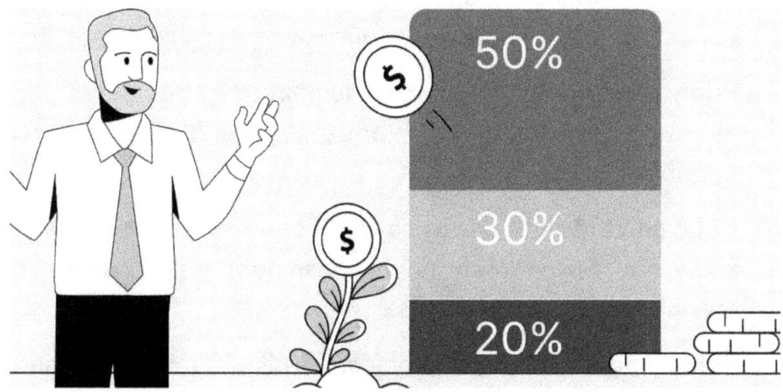

Figure 5

The 50-30-20 rule is a simple guideline to help manage money wisely by dividing it into three parts:

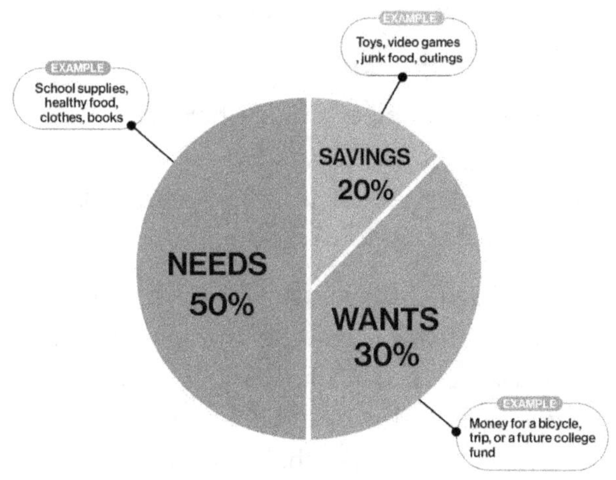

Figure 6

Why should one categorize with the 50-30-20 rule? The 50-30-20 rule, learned at an early age, is key to helping children develop strong financial habits that will last a lifetime. Here's the outcome of learning this fun concept early:

➢ **Budgeting Skills:** One learns to manage money efficiently, which sets the foundation for financial discipline later in life.

➢ **Prioritization:** It helps them understand that not everything they want can be bought immediately, and they need to prioritize their spending.

➢ **Delayed Gratification:** By saving money, one learns to wait and work toward larger, more meaningful goals instead of making impulsive purchases.

➢ **Preparedness for Emergencies:** Life is unpredictable, and having extra money saved up can help in tough times.

How Parents Can Help

Parents play a crucial role in helping children understand and implement the 50-30-20 rule. Here are some strategies that can be used to guide children:

1. **Use Real-Life Examples:** Explain how you manage family expenses using the same rule. For example, tell them how you allocate money for rent (a need), a family outing (a want), and a savings account for emergencies or vacations.

2. **Encourage Regular Savings:** Whenever children receive pocket money, festival gifts, or money from chores, help them set aside a portion for savings. Discuss short-term goals (like buying a toy or book) and long-term goals (like saving for a bicycle or even their college fund).

3. **Reward Good Financial Behavior:** When your child successfully follows the 50-30-20 rule, offer praise or small rewards to reinforce the importance of smart financial decisions. This positive reinforcement makes saving money feel rewarding.

4. **Create a Visual Tracker:** Use charts or apps like Alpha Wallet (if they are tech-savvy) to track their spending, savings, and how they allocate their earnings. Visual trackers give children a clear understanding of how much they are saving and spending on needs and wants. Refer to the mobile application Stash for a digital tool to accomplish this.

Activities for Parents and Children

Here are some fun and interactive activities that can be done at home to reinforce the 50-30-20 rule:

Activity 1: The Needs vs. Wants Sorting Game

Objective: To help children understand the difference between needs and wants.

What You Need: Magazines or store catalogues, two large boxes or bags labeled "Needs" and "Wants," scissors.

How to Play:

1. Sit with your child and go through the magazines or catalogues. Cut out pictures of items that are typically considered needs and wants (e.g., food, toys, clothes, gadgets).

2. Ask your child to place each item into either the "Needs" or "Wants" box.

3. Once done, discuss why certain items are categorized as needs and others as wants. This helps children build critical thinking skills around decision-making. Encourage them to consider whether some of the "Wants" could wait, teaching them the value of patience and prioritization.

Activity 2: The 50-30-20 Challenge

Objective: To practice using the 50-30-20 rule with real or play money.

What You Need: Play money (or small amounts of real money if your child receives pocket money), three labeled jars: Needs, Wants, and Savings, and a goal chart for savings (optional).

How to Play:

1. Give your child a fixed amount of money (e.g., ₹100) and explain that they need to divide it based on the 50-30-20 rule:

    -   ₹50 for needs.

    -   ₹30 for wants.

    -   ₹20 for savings.

2. Ask your child to place the correct amounts into each jar.

3. Discuss what they plan to do with their needs, wants, and savings. For example, they might decide to buy school supplies with their needs money, save for a toy with their wants money, and save long-term for a bicycle with their savings.

4. Create a goal chart for savings where they can track their progress. Each time they add to their savings jar, they can color in a portion of the chart.

5. The same can be accomplished using the Stash Mobile application.

Activity 3: The Weekly Budget Planner

Objective: To help children plan their spending and saving over a week.

What You Need: A simple weekly budget template, pen or pencil.

How to Play:

1. At the beginning of each week, sit down with your child and discuss how much money they will have for the week (e.g., pocket money or chore earnings). This will set the stage for making conscious decisions about their finances.

2. Help them fill out the budget planner by estimating how much they will spend on needs, wants, and how much they will save. Teach them to be realistic and mindful about how much to allocate for each category, encouraging them to think ahead.

3. At the end of the week, review the budget together to see if they followed it. Talk about how they can improve or reward them for sticking to their plan.

Activity 4: Trip to the Store – Learning to Prioritize

Objective: To teach children how to prioritize spending and make smart choices between needs and wants.

What You Need: A trip to a local store, a small amount of money (e.g., ₹ 100-200) for your child to spend.

How to Play:

1. Give your child a fixed amount of money and tell them they can choose to spend it on whatever they like. This gives them the freedom to make their own decisions while learning about budgeting.

2. At the store, help them categorize their choices into needs and wants. For example, if they choose a notebook, it's a need. If they choose a chocolate bar, it's a want.

3. Encourage them to think about whether they want to spend all their money on wants or save some for something bigger in the future.

4. After the store visit, discuss how they felt about their choices. Did they prioritize needs? Did they have any regrets about spending on wants?

CHAPTER - 5

Budget Like a Boss:
Your Money, Your Rules

Figure 7

Budgeting is about planning how to use money wisely. It's a skill children can learn early, preparing them to manage bigger finances in the future.

As children grow, introducing them to budgeting becomes essential. Parents can work with their children to create a straightforward budget that allocates funds for savings, spending, and charitable contributions. Understanding how to track expenses is crucial for successful budgeting, allowing children to make informed financial decisions. I guess that means you can now say **your piggy bank's about to become the coolest math teacher ever!**

Budgeting can be integrated into various subjects, reinforcing its practical applications in daily life.

What is a budget?

A budget helps you understand how much money you have and how much you're spending. It's like a plan for your money.

Steps to create a simple budget

1. **List your income:** This is the money you receive, such as gifts, allowances, or earnings from chores.

2. **List your expenses:** Write down everything you spend money on, like toys, snacks, or games.

3. **Track your savings:** Note how much you're saving for future needs.

Detailed Activity: Budgeting Role-Play Game – "The Budget Planner"

Objective: To help children learn how to allocate a fixed amount of money for different expenses while balancing their savings.

Materials needed

➢ Play money or tokens.

➢ A simple budget template with categories like "Food," "Toys," "Savings," and "Entertainment."

➢ A list of items with prices (e.g., ice cream ₹ 50, a toy car ₹ 100, movie tickets ₹ 60, a book ₹ 80).

Instructions

1. **Set Up the Scenario:** Tell your child they have ₹200 to spend for the week. They need to decide how to allocate it across different categories: essentials (food), savings, and fun (toys and entertainment).

2. **Present Options:** Show them a list of items they can "purchase" along with their prices. Include both needs (e.g., lunch for school) and wants (e.g., a toy or game).

3. **Role Play:** The parent acts as the "shopkeeper" and the "banker." The child comes to purchase items and manages their budget.

4. **Decision Time:** Encourage your child to:

   - Spend on one or two essential items.

   - Allocate a portion to savings.

   - Decide which fun items they want most and whether they can afford them.

5. **Review the Outcome:** At the end of the game, discuss:

   - How much money they have left.

   - Whether they spent wisely.

   - How saving a part of their money will help them in the future.

Extension: As a bonus, you can include "unexpected events" where they might need extra money for emergencies (e.g., a sudden repair cost for a bicycle). This will teach them the importance of an emergency fund.

Learning outcomes

This game helps children:

➢ Understand the difference between needs and wants.

➢ Practice prioritizing expenses.

➢ Learn the value of saving and planning for unexpected situations.

CHAPTER - 6

Oops to Aha!:
Turning Mistakes Into Money Smarts

Figure 8

Everyone makes mistakes, especially when it comes to managing money. However, learning from those mistakes early can help children avoid bigger financial problems later in life. This chapter discusses some common money mistakes children and teens make and offers practical strategies to avoid them.

Common Financial Mistakes

1. **Spending Everything at Once:** It's easy to spend money as soon as it's earned or received. Children may feel the urge to buy a toy, game, or treat immediately without thinking about saving for future needs.

    How to Avoid: Encourage children to follow the 50-30-20 rule (50% needs, 30% wants, 20% savings) and practice self-control by waiting before making purchases. Creating a sense of patience with money can also foster a deeper appreciation for its value. Additionally, involving them in financial decisions around the house, such as budgeting for a family outing, will reinforce these lessons.

2. **Not Saving for the Future:** Children often don't think about future needs, focusing instead on what they want now. This can lead to a habit of not saving enough.

    How to Avoid: Help children set specific savings goals, whether for something small (like a new game) or long-term (like college or a big trip). Teach them the power of compound interest and how money grows when saved over time.

3. **Not Keeping Track of Spending:** When children don't track their spending, they often run out of money without realizing where it went. This can lead to confusion and frustration when they discover they've spent more than they intended, with no idea where it all went.

    How to Avoid: Introduce simple budgeting tools, such as a notebook or an app like Alpha Wallet, to track earnings, spending, and savings. Make it a habit for them to log their expenses each day, so they stay aware of their financial decisions.

4. **Borrowing and Not Repaying:** Sometimes children might borrow money from family or friends and forget to pay it back. This can create bad habits around debt, affecting their relationships and financial well-being.

   How to Avoid: Teach children to borrow responsibly, and if they do, make sure they repay the money on time. Setting rules for borrowing within the family can also help. Discuss the importance of trust and how borrowing without repaying can damage relationships.

5. **Impulse Buying:** Children may feel tempted to buy things on impulse, like a new toy or gadget, without considering whether they really need it or if it's a smart financial choice.

   How to Avoid: Encourage children to ask themselves, "Do I really need this, or can I wait?" before making any purchase. This simple question can help them assess whether a purchase is truly necessary. Creating a "wish list" can help them think about their wants more carefully.

Activities for Parents and Children

➢ **Activity 1: Spot the Mistake – Storytime**

➢ **Objective:** Help children learn from relatable financial errors and develop problem-solving skills in managing money.

➢ **Instructions:**

   1. Create a short story about a fictional character (e.g., Alex) who overspends their allowance or skips saving for important needs.

   2. Pause the story at key decision points and ask, "What do you think Alex should do now?"

3. Discuss how the character's actions led to specific consequences, and highlight the lessons to be learned.

This activity makes financial lessons more engaging by turning them into a relatable and interactive story. It shows children how their choices can have real-life consequences, making them think twice before making impulsive decisions.

➢ **Activity 2: The "Impulse Buy" Game**

➢ **Objective:** Teach about resisting impulse purchases.

➢ **Instructions:**

1. Role-play a shopping scenario where parents pretend to be store vendors, offering tempting but unnecessary items. For example, offer the child a toy they don't need, or an extra snack that isn't part of their planned shopping list.

2. The child has to decide whether to "buy" or save their money for something more important. Encourage them to pause before making the decision and reflect on whether the item is truly needed or just an impulse buy.

This game teaches children the valuable skill of self-control and how to make thoughtful, informed decisions in real-life situations.

➢ **Activity 3: Parent-Child Reflection: "My Worst Money Mistake"**

➢ **Purpose:** Foster open, honest discussions about financial errors.

➢ **Instructions:**

- Parents share a real-life money mistake and what they learned from it.

- Encourage the child to share any small mistake they've made (like losing money or overspending on snacks).

By sharing personal experiences, parents help normalize financial errors as part of the learning process. This activity promotes a growth mindset, teaching children that mistakes don't have to define their financial future—they are simply opportunities for growth and better decision-making.

CHAPTER - 7

Chore Hustle:
Earn It, Love It

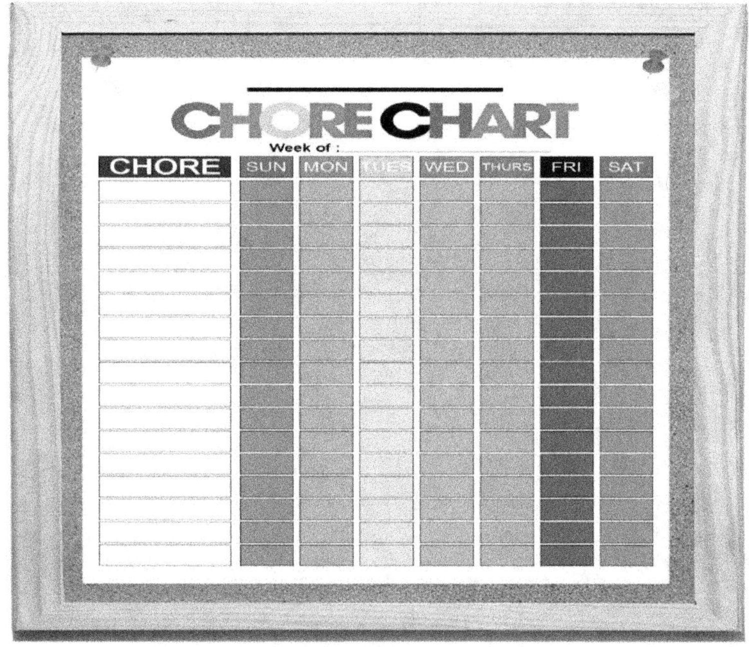

Figure 9

Sometimes, creating value is always better than just learning how to make money. Children often receive allowances or pocket money from their parents, but to teach the value of money, parents can link this to doing chores and tasks. By rewarding children for their work, they learn that money is earned through effort and responsibility. This not only helps around the house but also instills a strong work ethic in kids.

Why Tying Chores to Money is a Good Idea

➢ **Teaches Responsibility:** When children contribute to household tasks, they understand that being a part of the family comes with responsibilities.

➢ **Encourages Saving and Spending:** Earning money gives kids a sense of independence. They can decide how to spend or save their earnings.

➢ **Builds Financial Literacy:** Children start to connect effort with reward, which lays the foundation for budgeting and managing finances.

Creating a Chore Chart

It's important to create a fair system where certain chores have a specific value. This helps children see how their efforts can grow their earnings.

Here's a sample table of common chores and their suggested rewards:

Chore	Suggested Reward
Helping a sibling	₹ 50
One day gadget free	₹ 200
Watering plants	₹ 20
Planning an activity for the family	₹ 100
Effort towards learning a new skill	₹ 200
Feeding/Walking pets	₹ 15
Completing homework early	₹ 20

Parents can customize this list based on what works for their family, ensuring that it's both fair and motivating. The key is to align the reward with the task, so children understand the connection between effort and reward. A win-win for both!

Activities for Parents and Children

Activity 1: "The Busy Bee Earns Her Honey"

Ria was always asking her parents for money to buy things like candies and toys. One day, her mother said, "Ria, if you want to earn money, you can help me around the house."

Her mother created a chore chart, and every time Ria finished a task, she earned a few rupees. At first, Ria didn't think it was much, but by the end of the month, she had saved up ₹200! She realized that her hard work had paid off, and now she could buy the things she had been wanting for a long time.

Activity 2: The Value of Consistent Earnings

Parents can encourage children to save part of their chore earnings each week. It teaches them the importance of delayed gratification. When children work towards a long-term goal, like saving for a special toy or an outing, they understand the value of patience and planning.

Over time, they will see the benefits of their savings grow, which reinforces the idea that good things come to those who plan and save.

CHAPTER - 8

Big Ideas, Small Steps:
Kidpreneurs in the Making

While chores are a great way for children to earn money, they aren't the only option. Many young entrepreneurs start small businesses or find creative ways to earn money doing what they love. This chapter will inspire children with ideas that encourage them to think outside the box and explore new opportunities. Young money makers are about to turn playtime into payday!

Figure 10

Why Starting a Business Early is Beneficial

Starting a business at a young age teaches children many valuable lessons:

➢ **Responsibility:** Running a small business requires commitment, consistency, and follow-through.

➢ **Time Management:** Balancing school, extracurricular activities, and their business teaches children how to prioritize tasks and use their time wisely.

➢ **Customer Service:** Interacting with customers, even if they are just neighbors or family members, teaches communication skills and the value of good service.

➢ **Money Management:** Earning money from a business helps understand costs, profits, and savings.

Low Cost Kid-Friendly Business Ideas

1. **Lemonade Stand:** A classic business that teaches buying supplies, setting prices, and making profits.

2. **Pet Sitting or Dog Walking:** Children who love animals can offer to take care of pets when neighbors or friends are away.

3. **Digital Art and Design Business:** Create and sell digital illustrations, custom avatars, or graphics using tools like Canva or Procreate. Sell on platforms like Etsy or Fiverr.

4. **Drop Shipping Store:** Start an online store for trendy products like toys or accessories using Shopify. No inventory needed—partner with suppliers like Printful.

5. **Social Media Management:** Help local businesses manage social media by creating posts and responding to comments. Leverage skills on platforms like Instagram.

6. **Content Creator/YouTuber:** Start a channel on YouTube or TikTok focusing on gaming, crafts, or tutorials. Earn through ads, sponsorships, or merchandise.

7. **Virtual Tutoring or Skill Sharing:** Teach skills like coding, music, or gaming tricks to peers online. Use platforms like Zoom or Outschool to connect with learners.

How to Get Started

To start any business, here's a simple guide:

1. **Choose a business idea:** Pick something that the child enjoys doing or is skilled at.

2. **Plan and set goals:** Decide what they want to earn and how much time they can spend on the business.

3. **Get the word out:** Let family, friends, and neighbors know about the business. Flyers, social media with parental help, and word of mouth are great ways to spread the news.

4. **Save and reinvest:** Save part of earnings and reinvest in their business, such as buying better supplies or learning new skills.

Example: If a child earns ₹500 from a lemonade stand, they might save ₹100, spend ₹50 on supplies for the next stand, and use the remaining ₹350 for their wants or savings goals.

Activities for Parents and Children

- ➤ **Activity 1:** Market Research Walk

- ➤ **Purpose:** Teach children the importance of understanding demand and identifying opportunities.

- ➤ **Instructions:**

  - Take a walk around your neighborhood, visit a local event, or attend a community event.

  - Observe potential opportunities: Is there a need for a lemonade stand? A car-washing service?

  - Engage the child in a discussion: What needs or problems did they notice? How can they create a solution to meet these needs?

- ➤ **Activity 2:** Build a Business Plan Together

- ➤ **Purpose:** Introduce the basics of planning before starting any venture.

- ➤ **Instructions:**

  - Use a simple template:

    - **What I'll Do:** (e.g., bake cookies to sell at school events).
    - **What I'll Need:** (e.g., ingredients, tools, packaging).
    - **Who I'll Sell To:** (e.g., classmates, neighbors).

- ➤ **Discuss costs:** Break down expenses like supplies and tools.

- ➤ **Calculate potential earnings:** Show how much profit they can make by subtracting costs from earnings.

Activity 3: Create a Mini Advertisement

➢ **Purpose:** Teach the basics of marketing and how to attract customers.

➢ Instructions:

- Help the child design posters, flyers, or social media posts for their business idea.

- Use tools like Canva for digital designs or keep it simple with paper, markers, and stickers.

- **Encourage creativity:** Discuss how to grab people's attention with catchy slogans or vibrant visuals.

- **Role-play customer interactions:** Practice explaining their business idea to family members or friends.

- **Discuss distribution:** Where will they display their advertisements? What's the best way to spread the word?

By participating in these activities, children learn practical skills like observation, planning, and communication, setting them on the path to becoming thoughtful and confident entrepreneurs.

CHAPTER - 9

Goal Getters:
Turning Dreams Into Dollars

While chores are a great way for children to earn money, they aren't the only option. Many young entrepreneurs start small businesses or find creative ways to earn money doing what they love. This chapter will inspire children with ideas that encourage them to think outside the box and explore new opportunities. Young money makers are about to turn playtime into payday!

Figure 11

Teaching children the importance of saving can instill good financial habits from a young age. Parents can introduce savings by providing a piggy bank or a transparent jar for spare change. This simple act creates a visual connection, helping them see their progress and understand the value of every coin they add. Encouraging children to set savings goals, such as saving for a toy or special treat, can motivate them as they watch their funds grow.

This practice helps them learn the value of delayed gratification, as they distinguish between needs and wants.

One of the most important things to learn is how to set financial goals. Whether it's saving for a toy or for college, setting goals helps them understand the value of long-term planning. It's not just about money—it's about learning discipline, focus, and perseverance.

How to Set SMART Goals

SMART goals are:

➢ Specific

➢ Measurable

➢ Achievable

➢ Relevant

➢ Time-bound

For example, if a child wants to save ₹1,000 in 6 months, they can break it down into smaller monthly goals, such as saving ₹167 each month. By tracking their progress regularly, they can see how every small step brings them closer to achieving their dream.

Story: "The Journey of Ryan: From Toy Reviewer to Media Mogul

At just 3 years old, Ryan loved watching videos of kids reviewing toys on YouTube. One day, he asked his parents, "Why can't I do that?" His parents decided to give it a try and started recording Ryan unboxing and playing with toys. They uploaded the videos to a channel they named Ryan's World.

At first, it was just a fun family project, but soon, Ryan's enthusiasm, creativity, and charm began to attract millions of viewers. By the time he was 6 years old, his channel had become one of the most-watched YouTube channels in the world. The young star's journey showed that passion, combined with a solid plan, can lead to extraordinary success.

With fame came challenges, and Ryan's parents decided to teach him the importance of **goal setting** to ensure his success would have long-term benefits. Together, they outlined both **short-term and long-term goals** to guide his efforts.

Short-Term Goals

Ryan and his parents identified small, achievable objectives:

1.   Improve his content by reviewing new and innovative toys.

2.   Create fun, educational videos that children would love.

3.   Save a portion of his earnings for personal expenses like new toys or hobbies.

Long-Term Goals

As Ryan grew older, his family emphasized planning for his future:

1. Save a significant portion of his earnings for college.

2. Expand beyond YouTube into a full-fledged brand, including merchandise, TV shows, and books.

3. Use part of his income to give back to causes like children's education and healthcare.

Ryan worked toward his short-term goals one step at a time, gaining confidence and learning how each small action contributed to something bigger. Over the years, he achieved his long-term goals as well, building a global brand and securing a bright future for himself.

Activities for Parents and Children: Reinforcing Goal Setting

Here are activities for parents and children to reinforce the concept of goal setting:

1. **Start with a Dream:** Ask your child to think of something they really want, like a toy, book, or special experience.

2. **Break It into Steps:** Calculate the cost and set smaller saving milestones to reach the ultimate goal.

3. **Visualize Progress:** Create a fun progress tracker together, like a savings thermometer, where they can color in sections as they save.

4. **Celebrate Success:** Acknowledge every milestone, no matter how small, to keep their motivation alive.

This hands-on approach not only teaches children the mechanics of goal-setting but also makes the journey enjoyable and rewarding.

CHAPTER - 10

Fail, Rise, Thrive:
Lessons from Entrepreneurs

The road to success is rarely smooth. Many entrepreneurs experience failure before they find success. Sharing stories of business leaders who faced setbacks and rose again can inspire children to persevere when they face their own challenges in life.

Why Stories of Failure Matter

Hearing about failures helps understand that mistakes are a part of learning and growing. Success doesn't always come immediately, and that's okay. What matters is the ability to keep going and learn from setbacks. These stories act as powerful reminders that greatness is often born out of adversity.

DHIRUBHAI AMBANI (INDIA)

Dhirubhai Ambani started his career as a small trader selling spices and polyester yarn in Mumbai. His early business ventures faced many challenges, including market crashes and skepticism from others. However, Ambani never gave up. He learned from each failure, and over time, he built Reliance Industries, which is now one of India's largest companies.

His persistence and belief in himself were key to his success.

STEVE JOBS (USA)

Steve Jobs is famous for co-founding Apple, but many people don't know that he was once fired from his own company. After being forced out, Jobs could have given up, but he didn't. Instead, he used the time to create new companies like Pixar and NeXT. Years later, he returned to Apple and transformed it into one of the most successful tech companies in the world. Jobs' story shows that failure is not the end, but often a step toward something even greater.

His journey underscores the idea that resilience and vision can turn even the toughest moments into opportunities for reinvention.

KIRAN MAZUMDAR-SHAW (INDIA)

Kiran Mazumdar-Shaw faced skepticism when she started Biocon, a biotech company, in the late 1970s. At the time, there were very few women in the field, and raising money was incredibly difficult. Despite numerous obstacles, she persisted. Today, Biocon is one of the leading biotech firms in India, and Kiran is celebrated as one of

the most successful entrepreneurs in the country.

Her determination broke barriers and set an inspiring example for future generations, proving that hard work and persistence can rewrite the rules of any industry.

WALT DISNEY (USA)

Before creating Disney Studios, Walt Disney faced multiple bankruptcies and failed ventures. His first animation company didn't take off, and he even lost the rights to one of his first popular characters. However, he continued to innovate and dream big. Eventually, Disney went on to create Mickey Mouse and build an entertainment empire, proving that failure is just a stepping stone.

His story shows that no matter how tough the challenges, imagination and determination can turn failures into success..

These stories demonstrate important lessons:

➢ **Perseverance:** Don't give up after setbacks.

➢ **Learning from Mistakes:** Each failure is an opportunity to grow.

➢ **Innovation:** Stay open to new ideas, even when things aren't going as planned.

➢ **Value Creation:** When you learn to create value, money will follow.

➢ **Humility:** Treat your team with the respect each member deserves.

Activity for Kids

Purpose: Inspire children to embrace resilience and learn from real-world examples of overcoming failure.

1. **Choose an Entrepreneur:** Ask your child to pick an entrepreneur they admire. It could be someone they've read about in this chapter or a local businessperson they know.

2. **Research Their Journey:** Guide your child to find information about the challenges this entrepreneur faced. Discuss how these setbacks shaped their path to success.

3. **Create a Storyboard:** Encourage your child to visually map out the entrepreneur's story on a piece of paper:

   - **Beginning:** What motivated them to start their journey?

   - **Challenge:** What was the major obstacle they encountered?

   - **Triumph:** How did they overcome the challenge, and what did they achieve?

4. **Present and Reflect:** Have your child present their storyboard and reflect on the lessons they learned from the entrepreneur's story.

This activity not only enhances storytelling and research skills but also instills the value of resilience in the face of challenges.

CHAPTER - 11

Stash Wallet:
A Smart Way to Track Your Money

Stash is a mobile application designed for parents and children to track and manage money without the need for actual cash exchange. The app helps children understand basic personal finance concepts, categorize spending as 'Needs' or 'Wants,' and automatically allocate a portion of money to savings.

The Stash mobile application is available on both Android and iOS. This tool helps children and parents record transactions without using real money. Whether it's a gift from a relative, money earned from chores, or pocket money, Stash helps track it all.

Children can withdraw money and categorize it as a need or a want. The parent approves and disburses the funds. There are goals that can be set and financial literacy education available on this app.

How Stash Works

➢ **Categorize Money:** Children can divide their funds into three key areas: needs, wants, and savings. This simple exercise helps them understand the value of prioritization.

➢ **Automate Savings:** A unique feature of Stash is its automatic savings rule, where 20% of all deposited money is set aside and locked in savings. This teaches children the importance of building a financial cushion and the discipline of saving. These ratios can be changed by the users.

➢ **Interactive Learning:** Stash isn't just about tracking money. The app includes learning resources, FAQs, quizzes, and financial tips to build a strong foundation in finance.

This app is perfect for kids to practice managing their money before they start using real bank accounts.

Features of Stash Wallet for Families

Stash makes it easy for parents and children to implement everything they have read in this book.

Transaction Recording

Figure 12

➢ **Transaction Tracking:** Users (parents or children) can record new transactions such as deposits, withdrawals, or completed chores. Parents must approve withdrawals.

➢ **Chores and Rewards tracking :** Parents can assign chores to children with a specified reward amount. Upon completion, money is automatically added to the child's account.

Financial Goals

➢ **Set Goals:** Children can set financial goals (e.g., saving for a bicycle). Parents can set parameters such as maximum goal amounts.

➢ **Progress Tracking:** Display a progress bar showing how close the child is to achieving their goal, with a countdown timer to any deadlines.

Stock Market Simulator

➢ **Stock Market Introduction:** Children can learn the basics of stock markets using simulated investments in stocks or funds.

➢ **Virtual Portfolio:** Create a mock investment portfolio where children can "invest" virtual money to understand how the stock market works.

➢ **Tracking Performance:** Show simulated performance of investments to help children understand risk and reward.

Learning Resources

➢ **Educational Content:** Provide articles, videos, quizzes, and FAQs tailored to teaching personal finance concepts like saving, investing, budgeting, and more.

Figure 13

➢ **Parental Guides:** Additional resources for parents on how to teach personal finance at home.

Balance Management

➢ **Total Balance View:** Displays a visual breakdown of the child's total balance across the Needs, Wants, and Savings categories (50% Needs, 30% Wants, 20% Savings).

➤ **Automatic Savings:** 20% of all deposits are automatically allocated to savings, which are locked and cannot be withdrawn.

➤ **Manual Withdrawals:** Children can request withdrawals categorized as Needs or Wants. Parents approve these requests.

CHAPTER - 12

Banking 101: Your First Step to Financial Freedom

What is a Bank?

A bank is like a business — a place where people and companies keep their money, instead of stashing it in a piggy bank at home. A bank can offer services and financial products, just like a store does. It is a place where you can deposit your money and withdraw it when needed. Banks also give loans for businesses.

Opening a bank account for children is a great way to learn about managing money. Many banks offer **minor accounts** that children can use under the supervision of their parents.

Figure 14

Steps to Open a Bank Account

1. **Choose the right bank:** Look for banks specifically offering minor accounts with features like no minimum balance, parental controls, and learning resources. Research and compare options to find one that aligns with your child's needs.

2. **Visit the bank:** Parents and children can visit the bank to open the account together. This makes it an interactive experience and helps them feel involved in the process. It's also a great opportunity to introduce them to how banks operate.

3. **Deposit money:** Start by depositing a small amount of money that children can watch grow over time.

4. **Use the account:** Show them how to check their balance and encourage them to set savings goals.

KYC: What and Why?

Imagine you're opening a new club at school. You want to know who is joining because you want everyone to follow the club rules and keep things fun and safe. Just like that, when people want to open a bank account or a demat account, the bank or financial company also needs to know who they are. This process is called **Know Your Customer (KYC).**

KYC means checking who you are and making sure it's safe to trust you with important things like money or accounts. When you open a bank account, the bank wants to know who you are, where you live, and a bit about what you do. This helps them be sure they're doing business with a real person and not someone pretending to be you!

Why Is KYC Important?

1. **To Keep Everyone Safe:** Banks need to know who's using their services so they can keep everyone's money safe. If they know who you are, they can help protect your account from people who might want to take your money without permission.

2. **To Follow the Rules:** There are rules that banks and other companies have to follow to make sure people use money responsibly. By knowing who their customers are, they can make sure these rules are followed and help prevent problems.

3. **To Stop "Money Tricks":** Sometimes, people try to use fake names or do tricky things with money that are not allowed, like hiding where the money comes from. KYC helps banks catch these tricks and keep things fair for everyone.

How Does KYC Work?

When you, or a grown-up on your behalf, go to the bank to open an account, they will ask for some documents, such as:

➤ **A photo ID** like a passport or a driver's license, which helps them see who you are.

➤ **Proof of address** like a bill or a letter showing where you live.

Once the bank knows these details, they can open your account confidently. And now, they can help you save money or manage an account knowing they've done their part to keep it secure.

How Does a Bank Work?

When you deposit money into a bank, the bank uses some of that money to lend to others. But don't worry! Banks are required to keep a certain amount of cash on hand so that whenever you want to take money out, they'll have it ready for you.

Banks earn money in two key ways:

1. **Charging Interest on Loans:** When people or businesses borrow money, banks charge interest.

2. **Offering Special Services:** Banks provide additional services like investment accounts, credit cards, and financial planning, often charging fees for these.

Why It's Important to Use a Bank Wisely

Using a bank helps you manage your money responsibly. Saving, budgeting, and learning about interest can help one make good decisions for the future. While banks can help with big financial goals, it's also essential to avoid spending more than you have. Learning to save and spend carefully with a bank account can make a big difference in reaching your goals.

Remember: Saving and spending wisely today can lead to financial security tomorrow.

Types of Bank Accounts

1. **Minor Accounts:** A minor bank account is a savings or current account opened for individuals under 18, often with parental oversight. It helps children learn money management while providing access to basic banking services.

2. **Savings Account:** A safe place to store money while earning a little interest over time. Great for short-term goals or building emergency funds.

3. **Current Account:** An account used for everyday spending and payments, where you can write checks or use a debit card.

4. **Investment Accounts:** Some banks offer accounts for investing in things like stocks, bonds, or mutual funds to help you grow your money over time.

Click Smart:
Digital Money and Online Safety

Figure 15

Key Concepts:

Digital money is the money we use online instead of physical cash. It includes things like digital wallets, debit cards, and online payments.

➢ **Debit Cards:** Cards linked to your bank account that let you spend money directly from your savings or checking account.

➤ **Digital Wallets and Mobile Payments:** Tools like Apple Pay, Paytm, PayPal, or Google Pay make transactions easier and faster.

➤ **In-App Purchases:** Games and apps entice users to spend money, and it may be wise to set spending limits.

➤ **Digital Safety:** Protect personal information and avoid scams.

How to use money safely online:

➤ **Never Share Passwords or PINs:** Help kids understand the importance of keeping their passwords and PINs private, even from friends.

➤ **Recognize Secure Websites:** Teach them to look for "https" and a padlock symbol before entering any financial information online.

➤ **Avoid Clicking on Unknown Links:** There are phishing scams and that's why it's important not to click on links from unknown sources.

Parental control and supervision:

Parents play a vital role in ensuring their children's safety in the digital world:

➤ **Monitor Spending Habits:** Regularly check transaction history to make sure spending is wise and staying within limits.

➤ **Set Spending Limits:** Use apps or bank features to set daily or weekly spending limits on their digital wallets or cards.

➤ **Discuss Risks Openly:** There are dangers such as online fraud, overspending, and scams.

CHAPTER - 13

Stock Talk:
Investing Made Easy for Teens

The stock market is a fascinating place where people buy and sell shares of companies. While it may seem confusing at first, understanding it can be an exciting journey—and a great way for teens to start learning about investing and building wealth.

How Stock Markets Work

Imagine owning a small part of your favorite brand or company—like a piece of the magic that makes it successful! When you buy a stock, that's exactly what happens. Stocks, also known as shares, represent part ownership in a company.

Here's how it works:

➤ **Growth Potential:** If the company performs well and grows, the value of your stock increases. This means you could sell it for more than you paid.

➤ **Dividends:** Some companies reward their shareholders by paying small amounts of money called dividends, which represent a share of the company's profits.

➤ **Risk Factor:** If the company struggles, the value of your stock might go down, so it's important to be informed and cautious when investing.

The stock market, often called the equity market, is where these transactions happen. It's like a giant marketplace where people trade pieces of companies and share in their success—or challenges.

Why Should Teens Learn About the Stock Market?

Every profession in the world revolves around money. If you know how to earn and invest you are ahead of the entire pack.

Learning about the stock market early can help you understand how to build wealth and achieve goals in the future. Some teens even invest small amounts with the help of their parents, building smart habits early.

Key Concepts Every Teen Should Know

1. **Risk and Reward:** When you invest in stocks, there's a chance you can lose money if the stock's value goes down. This is called "risk." But there's also a chance for a "reward" if the stock's value goes up. The higher the risk, the higher the potential reward— but also the higher the potential loss!

Figure 16

2. **Diversification:** You might have heard the saying, "Don't put all your eggs in one basket." In the stock market, this means don't put all your money into one stock. Instead, spread it across different types of companies or industries. This way, if one stock doesn't do well, others might still perform, balancing your gains and losses.

3. **Long-Term Growth:** Stocks can go up and down every day, but over time, the market generally grows. Many experienced investors hold their stocks for years, letting the money grow slowly rather than trying to make fast money.

Pitfalls to Avoid in the Stock Market

1. **Following Fads:** It might be tempting to buy stocks that are popular on social media or because everyone seems to be talking about them. But just because a stock is popular doesn't mean it's a good investment. A stock might be overhyped and overpriced, leading to losses. Before investing in any company, take the time to research its financial health, business model, and why it might be a good choice.

2. **Over-Trading:** Some people think they can make fast money by constantly buying and selling stocks. This strategy, called "day trading," is very risky, especially for beginners. It requires deep market knowledge and can lead to significant losses. Additionally, frequent trading also means paying more fees, which can quickly add up and reduce your overall returns.

3. **Investing Money You Can't Afford to Lose:** One of the most important rules in the stock market is never to invest money you might need soon. The market goes up and down, so you might lose money if you have to sell quickly. Always use extra money that you're okay with setting aside for a while.

4. **Ignoring Fees and Costs:** Every time you buy or sell a stock, there's often a small fee involved. While these fees might seem small individually, they can add up significantly over time, eating into your returns. Research any fees with your brokerage to understand how much trading will cost.

5. **Expecting Instant Success:** Investing in stocks is not a get-rich-quick scheme. Successful investing often takes patience, discipline, and a long-term perspective. Some stocks might take years to grow in value. Getting rich overnight with stocks is rare and unrealistic. If you set realistic goals, you'll be more patient and successful over time.

Here are six key financial ratios that teens can look at when evaluating companies for potential investment. These ratios provide insights into a company's profitability, financial health, and how well it's managed:

1. **Price-to-Earnings (P/E) Ratio**

   - **What It Is:** The P/E ratio shows how much investors are willing to pay for a company's earnings. It's calculated by dividing the current share price by the earnings per share (EPS).

   - **Why It's Important:** This ratio helps teens understand if a stock is overvalued or undervalued compared to its earnings. A high P/E might mean that investors expect future growth, while a low P/E could suggest a bargain or a company facing challenges.

2. **Debt-to-Equity (D/E) Ratio**

   - **What It Is:** This ratio shows how much debt a company has compared to its equity. It's calculated by dividing the company's total liabilities by its shareholders' equity.

- **Why It's Important:** A high D/E ratio can indicate that a company is relying heavily on borrowed money, which could be risky if things go wrong. A lower ratio suggests a company is funded more by its owners than by debt, which is often seen as safer.

3. **Return On Equity (ROE)**

   - **What It Is:** ROE measures a company's profitability relative to shareholders' equity. It's calculated by dividing net income by shareholders' equity.

   - **Why It's Important:** ROE shows how effectively a company is using its investors' money to generate profit. A higher ROE generally means the company is using its resources well and could be a sign of a good investment.

4. **Return On Capital Employed (ROCE)**

   - **What It Is:** ROCE is a financial ratio that measures a company's profitability in terms of all of its capital. It's calculated by dividing a company's earnings before interest and taxes (EBIT) by capital employed (total assets – current liabilities).

   - **Why It's Important:** While ROE only analyzes profitability related to a company's shareholder equity, ROCE considers both debt and equity in analyzing a company's profitability. This performance analysis is important for companies with significant debt. A higher ROCE generally means the company is using its resources well and could be a sign of a good investment.

5. **Current Ratio (CR)**

- **What It Is:** The current ratio measures a company's ability to pay off its short-term debts with its short-term assets. It's calculated by dividing current assets by current liabilities.

- **Why It's Important:** This ratio helps teens understand if a company has enough resources to handle its bills in the near future. A current ratio over 1 indicates the company has more assets than liabilities, which is a good sign of financial stability.

6. **Net Profit Margin (NPM)**

- **What It Is:** This ratio shows how much profit a company makes from its revenue. It's calculated by dividing net income by total revenue.

- **Why It's Important:** A high net profit margin means the company keeps more of its revenue as profit after expenses. This can indicate strong management and cost control, both of which are positive for long-term investment.

Final Thoughts

The stock market can be exciting and a great way to grow your money, but it's important to be cautious and well-informed. Learning key financial ratios is essential. Start by researching companies, practicing patience, and avoiding common mistakes. Over time, with careful planning and learning, you can become a successful investor who knows how to grow wealth wisely.

The Future of Money – Cryptocurrencies and Digital Assets

Figure 17

> ➢ **Introduction to cryptocurrencies:**

Cryptocurrencies are digital or virtual currencies secured by cryptography, making them difficult to counterfeit or manipulate. They operate on decentralized networks called blockchains, which ensure transparency and security.

> ➢ **Should children be interested in crypto?**

Should children start learning about cryptocurrencies now or wait until later? While cryptocurrencies are an evolving space, it's a good idea for children to develop a basic understanding of them under parental guidance. They can safely explore this field by focusing on the foundational concepts without making actual investments.

➢ **Exploring digital assets:**

The digital economy is expanding beyond cryptocurrencies to include digital assets like non-fungible tokens (NFTs), which represent ownership of unique digital items such as art, music, or videos. Learning about these assets helps children understand how the financial world is changing and how technology is shaping the future.

Using Stock Simulators for Tweens

Parents can make the stock market more accessible to children by introducing them to stock simulators. These simulators let children trade stocks with fake money, so they can practice without any risk. Try apps like **Stock Trainer** or **Investopedia's Stock Simulator** to get started.

Activity: Practice Investing

1. Provide children with a list of well-known companies they recognize, like their favorite clothing brands, tech firms, or food chains.

2. Allow them to "invest" a fixed amount of fake money in these companies.

3. Track their investments over time to observe how their choices perform.

This activity not only teaches children about the stock market but also helps them develop analytical and decision-making skills in a fun, risk-free way.

CHAPTER - 14

Ads Unmasked:
How Media Shapes Your Choices

We are surrounded by advertisements every day – on TV, social media, billboards, and even in the apps we use. Children are often targeted by these ads, which try to convince them to buy things they may not need. This chapter helps children understand how advertising works and how to make smart decisions when they see ads.

Figure 18

What is Advertising?

Advertising is a way for companies to tell people about their products and encourage them to buy. To grab attention, companies often use bright colors, catchy music, fun characters, and exciting promises to make their products seem appealing.

How ads influence children's choices

➢ **Emotional Appeals:** Ads often create a sense of fun, excitement, or even happiness around their products, making children believe these items are essential for enjoyment or satisfaction.

➢ **Limited-Time Offers:** Ads sometimes create urgency by saying things like "Buy now, only available for a limited time!" This can push children to make quick decisions.

➢ **Social Influence:** Ads can make children feel like they need to buy something to fit in with their friends or be "cool."

Recognizing and questioning ads

It's important to recognize when we are being advertised to and to think critically about it. Here are some key questions they can ask themselves:

➢ Do I really need this, or do I just want it because I saw it in an ad?

➢ Is this product really as amazing as the ad makes it seem?

➢ Can I wait before buying it to see if I still want it later?

➢ Are there other ways to get what I need without buying this product?

How parents can help

Parents play a vital role in helping children navigate the world of advertising. Here are some strategies:

➢ **Discuss Advertisements Together:** Talk with your children about the ads they see and ask questions to encourage critical thinking, such as "Why do you think this ad uses that catchy jingle?" or "What is the company trying to achieve here?"

➢ **Set an Example:** Show your children how to evaluate purchases thoughtfully by modeling this behavior in your own spending habits.

➢ **Teach the Value of Money:** Help children understand that money is a limited resource and should be spent wisely on things that truly matter.

The goal is to make children aware that just because something is advertised doesn't mean it's necessary—or the best choice for them.

Patience Pays:
The Magic of Delayed Gratification

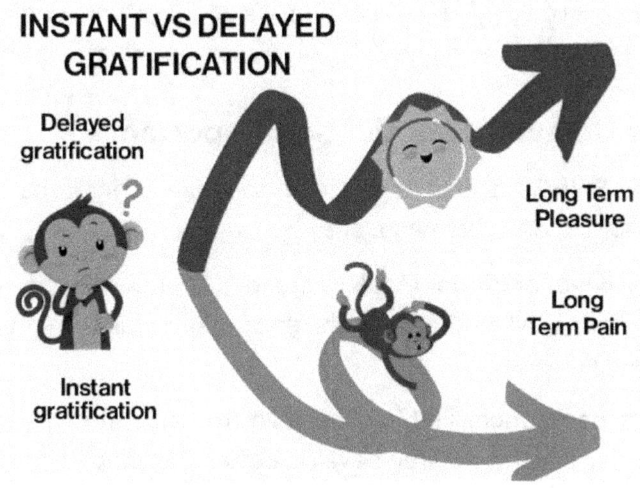

Figure 19

Delayed gratification means waiting to get something you want rather than taking it right away. This is an important concept for children to learn, as it helps them develop patience, self-control, and the ability to make smarter financial decisions over time.

Teaching children about delayed gratification involves encouraging critical thinking. By asking questions like, "Is this a necessity or just a desire?" This practice encourages them to evaluate their purchases carefully, helping to curb impulse buying. By emphasizing the importance of saving first, children learn to prioritize long-term financial security over immediate gratification

What is Delayed Gratification?

Imagine a child has enough money to buy a small toy now, but if they wait and save for a few more weeks, they could afford a much bigger toy. Choosing to wait and save for the bigger toy is an example of delayed gratification. It's about making choices that benefit the future instead of giving in to immediate desires.

Why is Delayed Gratification Important?

➢ **Builds Self-Control:** We can learn to manage our impulses and not act on every whim and desire.

➢ **Helps Save for Bigger Goals:** Instead of spending money on small items, waiting allows children to save for something more meaningful.

➢ **Improves Financial Habits:** The ability to wait before making a purchase helps children develop better spending habits for life.

Activities to Teach Delayed Gratification

1. **The Marshmallow Test:** This is a famous experiment where kids are given a marshmallow and told that if they wait 15 minutes without eating it, they can have two marshmallows. Try this experiment with your child to teach them about the rewards of waiting.

2. **Saving for a Goal:** Help your child set a bigger savings goal, such as buying a special toy or going on a trip. Encourage

them to wait until they have saved enough, rather than spending small amounts along the way.

3. **Create a Wishlist:** Instead of buying things on impulse, help your child create a list of items they want. Every month, review the list together to see if they still want those items or if their preferences have changed. This teaches them that desires can change over time and waiting can prevent regretful purchases.

How Parents Can Encourage Patience

Parents play a crucial role in fostering delayed gratification. Here's how you can help:

➤ **Be a Role Model:** Show your children how you wait and save for bigger goals, demonstrating the value of patience in your own life.

➤ **Encourage a Waiting Period:** Before buying something, suggest waiting for a specific period to see if they still want it.

➤ **Celebrate Savings Goals:** When your child achieves a savings milestone, celebrate their achievement to reinforce the positive outcomes of waiting.

Teaching children the value of delayed gratification equips them with essential life skills for financial success. With patience and practice, they'll learn that waiting can often lead to greater rewards.

CHAPTER - 16

Giving Back:
A Child's Heart is for Helping

Figure 20

Most people think of money as something to spend, save, or earn. But did you know that money can also be used to help others? Charity is a way to share what we have with people or causes that need support. By learning about charity, children can understand how money can make a positive impact, appreciate the value of every rupee, and build good habits for the future.

What is Charity?

Charity means giving something—like money, time, or items—to help others in need. When you donate to charity, you're using your money in a special way to make the world a better place. Charities work on many important things, like helping people who are hungry, taking care of animals, building homes for people, and even protecting the environment.

How Charity Helps You Understand Money

1. **Seeing the Value of Money:** When you donate to charity, you learn how much things cost and what a difference even a small amount can make. For example, if you donate to a food bank, you might see how $10 can buy several meals for someone in need. This builds an appreciation for the value of money and its potential to do good.

2. **Learning to Save for a Cause:** To make a donation, you might need to save a little bit of money from what you earn or receive as an allowance. Saving for a cause helps you understand how to set aside money with a specific goal in mind. It also shows that money isn't just about spending on things we want; it's also about setting goals that help others.

3. **Budgeting and Making Choices:** If you decide to donate some of your money to charity, you'll need to figure out how much you can afford to give while still having enough for other things, like savings or spending. This is called budgeting. Learning to budget teaches you how to balance different goals and priorities—a skill that will be useful throughout your life.

4. **The Joy of Giving:** When you give to charity, you experience the joy of knowing you've helped someone else. This shows that money can be more than just a way to buy things for ourselves—it can also bring happiness when it's used to help others. Studies show that people who give to charity often feel happier and more fulfilled, making charity a rewarding experience.

Ways to Get Involved in Charity

➢ **Donating Part of Your Allowance:** Set aside a small part of your allowance each week to donate to a cause you care about. This shows how saving a little can add up to a meaningful amount over time.

➢ **Fundraising Activities:** Organize a small fundraiser, like a lemonade stand, bake sale, or car wash, with friends or family. This not only raises money but also teaches valuable lessons in teamwork, planning, and earning for a purpose.

➢ **Donating Items:** Charity isn't always about giving money. You can also donate clothes, books, or toys you don't need anymore. This helps you understand that money and material items both have value when shared with others.

Understanding How Charities Use Money

Many charities share how they spend the donations they receive, often dividing funds between providing immediate help and investing in long-term projects. Learning how charities use donations helps you understand budgeting and the impact that wise spending can have on a community.

Why Charity is an Important Lesson

By participating in charity, you learn that money has many purposes. It's not only about earning and spending but also about helping, saving, and building communities. When you learn to give, you're also learning to be responsible, to plan, and to be grateful for what you have.

Ryan Hreljac – A Well of Hope

Ryan Hreljac was just six years old when he first learned in school that many people in Africa didn't have clean water to drink. The idea that children his age had to walk miles every day to fetch water—and often dirty water—moved him deeply. Ryan wanted to help, so he decided to raise money to build a well.

He began by doing chores around the house to earn money. Ryan raised his first $70 by cleaning his room, washing windows, and other small jobs. With a little help from his parents, Ryan reached out to a charity to see if he could donate this money to build a well. He soon found out that a well actually cost about $2,000! But Ryan didn't give up. He kept working, asking for donations, and sharing his story.

With the support of his family, friends, and community, Ryan eventually raised enough money to fund his first well in a Ugandan village. Today, Ryan's Wells has raised millions of dollars, providing clean water to hundreds of thousands of people in Africa. His story shows that even a small act, started by a child, can grow into something that changes lives.

Kavya Mehta –
Empowering the Homeless

When she was just eight years old, Kavya Mehta noticed people living on the streets in her Delhi neighborhood. Seeing homeless women struggling moved her to action. Kavya felt that everyone should have basic items to feel safe and clean, so she decided to help by creating "Kavya Cares" — a project that gives out "Care Bags" filled with essential items like soap, toothbrushes, socks, and hand sanitizer.

Kavya learned to sew with the help of her grandmother and began making strong, reusable tote bags to hold these items. She worked hard to fill each one with toiletries and other essentials and then handed them out to women in need. Kavya's project gained attention, and with community support, her efforts expanded. She has since distributed hundreds of Care Bags and inspired people around the world to make a difference in their own communities.

Today, Kavya speaks at events to inspire other young people to help those in need. Her message is clear: you don't have to wait until you're grown-up to change the world; you can start right where you are.

Money Lessons 101:
Should Schools Teach Finance?

Figure 21

Why Personal Finance Should Be Taught in Schools

Personal finance is a fundamental life skill that shapes how individuals navigate their financial lives, yet it is often overlooked in the formal education system. Many adults face financial difficulties, not because they lack knowledge in their professional fields but because they have never been taught how to manage money effectively. This gap in financial literacy can lead to issues such as debt, poor saving habits, and financial insecurity. Schools, as institutions responsible for holistic education, should take an active role in preparing children for the financial realities of adulthood.

In America, 22 states mandate financial education in high schools, underscoring the need for greater commitment from educational authorities to ensure equal opportunities for all students.

While in India, financial education in schools is still not widely emphasized. The lack of a formal personal finance curriculum often results in young adults entering the workforce without the skills needed to manage their finances. The emphasis on academic subjects like science, mathematics, and literature leaves little room for financial education. Yet, this is the very skill that can empower future generations to build stable financial futures.

Addressing these barriers is vital to creating a robust framework for teaching personal finance to children and teens, ultimately empowering them to navigate their financial futures with confidence and competence. Overall, the discourse surrounding personal finance education for youth is not without its controversies, particularly regarding the adequacy of existing programs and the responsibility of educational institutions to provide comprehensive financial literacy. As the dialogue continues, it is imperative to foster a supportive environment that prioritizes financial education, ensuring that children and teens are well-equipped to face the financial realities of adulthood.

Introducing personal finance as a subject in schools can provide students with the knowledge and tools necessary to make informed financial decisions throughout their lives. By learning about budgeting, saving, investing, and understanding credit, students can build a strong foundation of financial literacy from a young age. Schools are the ideal environment for teaching these skills because they reach all children, regardless of their background or family financial circumstances.

Teaching personal finance in schools is not just about understanding money; it's about fostering responsibility, independence, and future planning. For many children, school may be the only place where they are exposed to these concepts. Families may not always have the time, knowledge, or inclination to teach personal finance, making the role of teachers in this area crucial.

How Schools Can Introduce Personal Finance into Their Curriculum

To effectively teach personal finance, schools in India can integrate it into the curriculum in various ways:

1. **Stand-Alone Subject or Course**

   One approach is to introduce personal finance as a standalone subject in the school curriculum, similar to mathematics or science. This course could be introduced as early as middle school and could cover a range of topics such as:

   - **Budgeting and Money Management:** Understanding how to create a budget, track expenses, and differentiate between needs and wants.

- **Saving and Investing:** Exploring the importance of saving, the concept of interest, and the basics of investing.

- **Debt and Credit:** Teaching about loans, interest rates, and how to manage credit responsibly.

- **Taxes and Income:** Helping students understand how salaries, taxes, and deductions work.

- **Entrepreneurship:** Encouraging creative thinking and risk management by introducing basic entrepreneurial concepts.

To make the subject more engaging, schools could incorporate real-world simulations such as budgeting projects, mock investment portfolios, and saving challenges. Students could also engage in interactive learning experiences, such as running mock businesses or participating in games that simulate financial decision-making.

2. **Integrating Personal Finance into Existing Subjects**

   If creating a standalone course is not feasible, schools can integrate personal finance education into existing subjects like mathematics, social studies, or economics. For instance:

   - **In mathematics,** students can learn about percentages, interest rates, and budgeting as part of their arithmetic and algebra curriculum.

   - **In social studies,** students can explore the history of money, trade, and economic systems, linking financial literacy to broader economic principles.

   - **In economics,** personal finance topics such as supply and demand, credit, and investment could be woven into the study of macro and microeconomic systems.

3. Age-Appropriate Financial Education

It's essential to introduce financial education in an age-appropriate manner. For younger children in primary school, the focus can be on basic concepts like understanding the value of money, differentiating between needs and wants, and learning about saving. Teachers can use interactive activities, such as role-playing games or visual aids like savings jars, to make these ideas more relatable. For instance, teachers could organize classroom activities where students pretend to manage a small budget for a class party, helping them make decisions about spending, saving, and prioritizing. This hands-on approach fosters an early understanding of money as a resource that needs careful management.

As students advance to middle and high school, the curriculum can become more detailed, including topics like managing allowances, understanding bank accounts, and learning about financial products like loans and credit cards. High school students, on the brink of adulthood, should be exposed to more advanced concepts like taxes, investing, insurance, and retirement planning. By this stage, schools can offer elective courses in personal finance or make it a mandatory part of the senior curriculum to ensure every student graduates with a solid understanding of financial literacy. After all, it's not enough to merely know how to make money – students need to learn how to make it work for them in the long term.

4. Practical Application and Project-Based Learning

One of the most effective ways to teach personal finance is through hands-on, project-based learning. Schools can create opportunities for students to apply what they learn in real-life scenarios. For example:

➤ **Student-Led Financial Projects:** Schools can create school-wide projects where students manage a budget, plan an event, or even start small businesses, allowing them to see the real-world application of financial principles. These projects instill a sense of ownership and responsibility, showing students the direct impact of financial decisions on their environment.

➤ **Simulated Stock Market Games:** Students could participate in stock market simulators, learning the basics of investing and tracking the performance of virtual portfolios. This kind of simulation provides invaluable lessons in risk, timing, and strategic thinking without the consequences of real-world financial losses.

➤ **Field Trips and Guest Speakers:** Bringing in financial experts, such as bankers, entrepreneurs, or financial planners, can give students insights into how they might apply financial concepts in their careers. Field trips to local businesses, banks, or financial institutions can also provide valuable exposure to the workings of the financial world. These interactions broaden students' horizons and help them connect classroom lessons to real-world financial practices.

5. Collaborating with Parents

Schools can also engage parents in the financial education process by offering workshops or resources for families. This can help reinforce the lessons taught in class and encourage families to discuss financial literacy at home. Teachers can assign activities that involve both students and parents, such as creating a family budget or setting savings goals together.

The Benefits of Personal Finance Education in Schools

The long-term benefits of incorporating personal finance into the school curriculum are significant:

➢ **Empowerment and Confidence:** Financial literacy helps students feel more empowered and confident about managing their money. This sense of control reduces financial anxiety and fosters independence enabling students to make well-informed decisions about their finances.

➢ **Reduced Risk of Financial Mistakes:** By learning about money management early, students are less likely to make costly financial mistakes later in life, such as accumulating debt or failing to save for emergencies. This proactive approach sets them on the path to financial stability and security.

➢ **Preparation for Adulthood:** Schools prepare students for college and careers, but financial education ensures they are also ready for the financial responsibilities that come with adulthood, such as paying rent, managing loans, or investing in the future. This holistic preparation empowers students to navigate life's financial challenges confidently.

➢ **Economic Equity:** Providing financial education in schools helps level the playing field for students from all socioeconomic backgrounds, giving every child the opportunity to acquire these essential life skills, regardless of their family's financial knowledge.

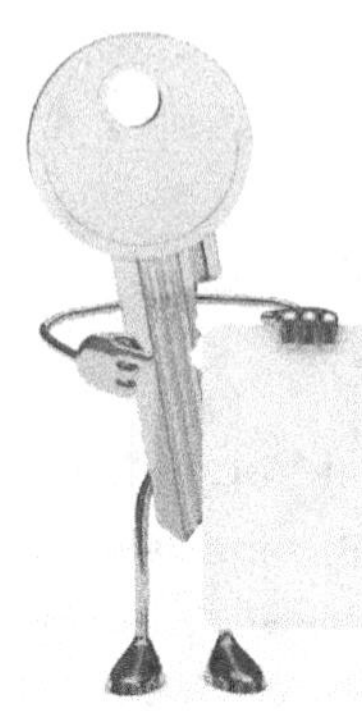

RECAP OF KEY FINANCIAL LESSONS

In this book, we've covered many important financial lessons that can help you build a strong financial foundation for the future. Let's quickly recap some of the key points we've discussed:

➢ **Save Like a Pro:** Start stashing your cash early—it's like planting seeds that grow into a money tree for your future!

➢ **Needs vs. Wants:** The Ultimate Cheat Code: Learn to tell the difference between must-haves and nice-to-haves. Use a mobile app like Stash to level up your spending game.

➢ **Budget Boss Moves:** Split your money into saving, spending, and sharing jars to stay on top of your cash flow and crush your money goals.

➢ **Patience Power-Up:** Waiting for something big instead of grabbing the first shiny thing? That's how you win at life—and money!

➢ **Earn It, Own It:** Crush those chores, earn rewards, and feel awesome knowing you're working hard for your goals.

➢ **Share the Love:** Giving back isn't just cool—it's a superpower! Even small donations can make a big difference in the world.

You have the power to make smart financial decisions every day!

Quiz: Challenge Your Money Knowledge!

1. **Savings**

    If you save $5 a week for a year, how much money will you have by the end of the year? Include an explanation of how you got your answer. ___________

2. **Delayed Gratification**

    Imagine you are offered $10 now or $50 if you wait for a month. What is this concept called, and why might waiting be the smarter choice? ___________

3. **Cryptocurrency**

    Name a key difference between cryptocurrencies like Bitcoin and traditional money. ___________

4. **Banks**

    If you deposit $500 in a bank account with an annual interest rate of 2%, how much will your money grow in one year? ___________

5. Investment Jargon

What is the purpose of "diversification" in investing, and how does it reduce risk? ___________

6. Budgeting

You have $100 to spend for the month, and you want to save 20%. How much will you save, and how much will you have left to spend? ___________

7. Risk and Reward

Why might investing in the stock market be riskier than keeping money in a savings account but also more rewarding over time? ___________

8. Interest

What is the difference between "simple interest" and "compound interest," and why does compound interest grow your money faster? ___________

9. Spending Wisely

Give an example of a situation where buying a cheaper product might cost you more in the long run. ___________

10. Giving Back

Explain how donating to a cause you care about can benefit both the people you're helping and yourself. ___________

1. **What does "inflation" mean?**

a) Prices of goods and services decrease over time

b) Prices of goods and services increase over time

c) Money becomes less important

2. **Which of these is a key feature of Bitcoin?**

a) It is controlled by banks

b) It uses blockchain technology to secure transactions

c) It loses value over time automatically

3. **If you save $5 a week for one year, how much will you have?**

a) $250

b) $260

c) $300

4. **What does "ROI" stand for in investing?**

a) Risk of Investment

b) Return on Investment

c) Rate of Interest

5. Which of these is an example of delayed gratification?

a) Spending all your money on a new video game immediately

b) Waiting to buy a bike after saving for six months

c) Borrowing money from a friend to buy snacks

6. What is a "smart contract" in cryptocurrency?

a) A type of digital wallet

b) A self-executing agreement on the blockchain

c) A subscription plan for buying crypto

7. Which of these describes "diversification" in investing?

a) Putting all your money in one type of investment

b) Spreading your investments across different types to reduce risk

c) Buying multiple shares of the same company

8. Imagine you find a $20 bill today. If you invest it at a 5% annual return, how much will it be worth in 10 years?

a) Around $30

b) Around $32.50

c) Around $50

9. What is "blockchain"?

a) A physical chain to lock your wallet

b) A secure digital ledger that records cryptocurrency transactions

c) A type of investment fund

10. What does it mean when a company "goes public"?

a) It starts selling shares on the stock market

b) It lets anyone work there

c) It gives all its profits to charity

Answers: Quiz 1

1. $260 (calculated as $5 x 52 weeks).

2. Delayed gratification; waiting often leads to a better outcome.

3. Cryptocurrencies are decentralized and not controlled by governments or banks.

4. $10 (2% of $500).

5. Diversification spreads investments, reducing the impact of a single loss.

6. Save $20 (20% of $100) and spend $80.

7. Stock markets are volatile, but over time, they often yield higher returns.

8. Compound interest earns interest on the initial deposit and on the interest earned.

9. Cheaper shoes that wear out quickly might cost more over time than durable ones.

10. Donating improves the lives of others and gives you a sense of fulfillment.

Answers: Quiz 2

1. b) Prices of goods and services increase over time

2. b) It uses blockchain technology to secure transactions

3. b) $260

4. b) Return on Investment

5. b) Waiting to buy a bike after saving for six months

6. b) A self-executing agreement on the blockchain

7. b) Spreading your investments across different types to reduce risk

8. b) Around $32.50

9. b) A secure digital ledger that records cryptocurrency transactions

10. a) It starts selling shares on the stock market

1. What are the three jars used to teach kids about money?

2. Can you explain the difference between needs and wants? Give one example of each.

3. What is the 50-30-20 rule? How do you use it?

4. Why is it important to start saving money early?

5. What does it mean to delay gratification? Can you share an example?

6. Name two ways kids can earn money at home through chores.

7. Are there any small business ideas that you can try which are not in the book?

8. Did you download the Stash mobile app and try it?

9. What are the benefits of keeping your money in a savings account instead of a piggy bank?

10. What does it mean to own a share of a company?

11. Why should you diversify your investments?

12. How can using a stock market simulator help you learn about investing?

13. How do advertisements try to influence your spending?

14. What are some questions you should ask yourself before buying something you saw in an ad?

15. Have you ever been influenced by a friend to buy or spend on something you did not want?

16. Why is it important to give back to others?

17. Can you name a cause or charity you would like to support and explain why?

18. Name one entrepreneur from the book who faced failure. What did they do to succeed?

19. Why is failure a good teacher?

20. What is a budget?

21. How can learning about money help you when you grow up?

22. Do you think everyone should learn about personal finance? Why or why not?

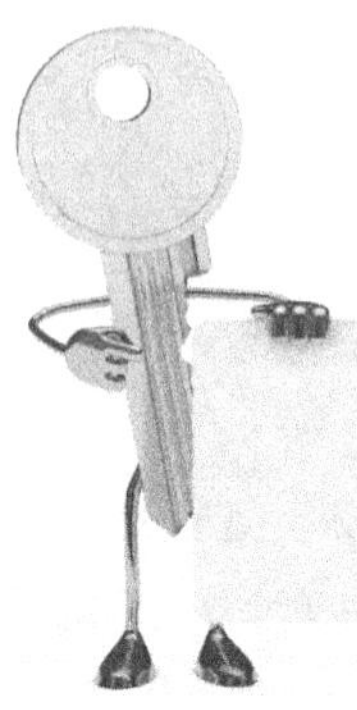

THE FUN'S NOT OVER LET'S TALK!

Thank you for picking up this book and completing this transformative journey with me!

I hope you've discovered powerful insights and gained the knowledge you need to take full control of your future.

Got Questions?

Need Clarity on Any Topic?

Want to Dive Deeper into Financial Journey?

I'm here for YOU!

Let's take it further together!

Schedule Your Personalized 1-2-1 Consultation and let's discuss your feedback, guidance, or a deeper dive into any concept, I'm excited to be a part of your growth.

Email: jshaurya380@gmail.com

@STASH.HQ

Shaurya Anand Jain

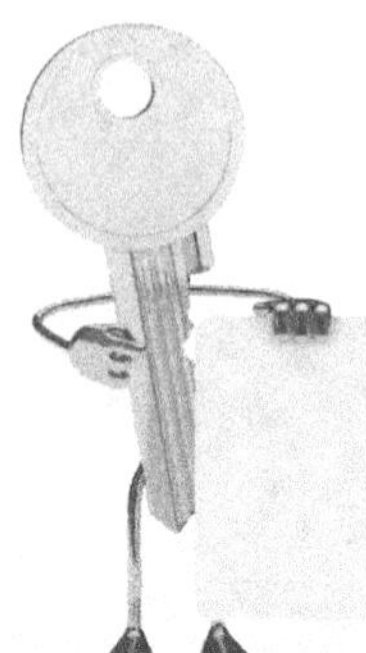

REFERENCES CITING

➤ https://thecollegepod.com/budgeting-for-teens/

➤ https://bettermoneyhabits.bankofamerica.com/en/personal-banking/teaching-children-how-to-budget

➤ https://www.moneywellth.com/knowledge/teaching-kids-about-financial-literacy-an-intro-guide-by-age/

➤ https://www.kidsmoney.org/parents/money-management/three-jar-method/

➤ https://www.nfcc.org/blog/teach-your-children-to-save-money-with-these-expert-tips/

➤ https://www.thebalancemoney.com/how-to-teach-your-teen-about-budgeting-4160105

➤ https://www.capitalone.com/bank/money-management/financial-tips/budgeting-for-teens/

➤ https://nationofcredit.com/teaching-financial-literacy-to-children-age-appropriate-strategies/

➤ https://www.investopedia.com/personal-finance/10-tips-teach-your-child-save/

➤ https://www.parents.com/parenting/money/family-finances/teaching-kids-about-money-an-age-by-age-guide/

- https://www.moneyprodigy.com/how-to-teach-budgeting/
- https://jasonfintips.com/financial-education-and-literacy-blog/what-to-teach-kids-about-money-a-comprehensive-guide-for-parents/
- https://savvymoneylessons.com/budgeting-tips-for-teens
- https://www.thepennyhoarder.com/budgeting/budgeting-for-kids/
- https://www.sofi.com/learn/content/budgeting-as-high-school-student/
- https://edcraft.io/blog/all-articles/step-by-step-financial-literacy-guide-for-kids
- https://www.creditkarma.com/financial-planning/i/budgeting-for-teens
- https://www.kidsmoney.org/teachers/budgeting/
- https://www.moneyprodigy.com/budgeting-for-kids/
- https://www.thebalancemoney.com/teach-kids-to-budget-money-454012
- https://www.themuse.com/advice/budgeting-for-teens
- https://ecosystemventures.in/2023/08/20/the-turnaround-story-of-cafe-coffee-day/?utm_source=chatgpt.com
- https://www.ryanswell.ca/about-us/our-story
- https://www.pexels.com/
- https://pixabay.com/

NOTES